QUEEN
UNLEASHED

Rise from Pain to Purpose
and Rediscover Yourself

Real life Transformational Story & Blueprint of
How to overcome Life's Challenges &
Rediscover yourself!

By

Gladness Katega

QUEEN UNLEASHED

Rise from Pain to Purpose and Rediscover Yourself

Real life Transformational Story & Blueprint of How to overcome Life's Challenges & Rediscover yourself!

ISBN - 978-1-80049-092-5

Printed in the United Kingdom

Published by Independent Publishing Network

TABLE OF CONTENTS

ACKNOWLEDGMENT

I give all Glory and Honour to God Almighty for his Grace and Mercy; I thank God for getting me through a terrible season of my life by allowing me to rise from pain to purpose. My Testing season has become a testimony that I can share my story and be a blessing to others that will benefit from hearing my victory.

The year 2019 was life-changing for me as my first daughter Amore Ojo passed on to Glory and I ended my marriage after 9 years of being in a mentally abusive relationship. I want to acknowledge my family for sticking by me through the most challenging time of my life. I would not have been able to stand back on my feet after a traumatic experience without the support of my mother – Margaret Ntare, My Sisters; Melanie, Georgase, Gratty, Grandy, Yolanda, Michelle and My Brother Gracious as well as my amazing friends Titilayo, Bree, Olive, Alice and Linda to name a few and all my aunties, uncles and cousins that stood by me in this season.

I dedicate this book to my first-born child in heaven, Amore Ojo as God told me and so it became that you are my Testimony. Also, I give special thanks of love to my other children Alana Ojo and Samuel Junior Ojo for giving me the strength to live every day, as your love makes my life complete. I also dedicate this book to Alana and Junior as a testament to the Glory of God in breaking the cycle of broken marriages in my family from now to their generation and beyond.

ABOUT THE BOOK

"QUEEN UNLEASHED"

This book "Queen Unleashed" is designed to release your inner Queen that lives inside of you that may be hidden away from limitation, negative experiences and life challenges and trauma such as domestic abuse. The book is created to help women discover their full potential and worth as God's precious creation breaking away from common society misconceptions of the identity of women.

The book is written based on a true story of a broken woman that rediscovered herself rising from pain into her purpose despite life's challenges after undergoing the loss of a child and divorce. The book is written to showcase the strength of a woman once she has known the truth about her value and worth and is equipped with the right information to help her concur her pain and overcome life's challenges.

"Queen Unleashed" will show you how to become a courageous woman who takes deliberate action to empower herself to achieve her goals. It will enable you to become a woman who is certain about her wants and has clarity about the direction she wants her life to take, it will show you the importance of understanding your life's purpose.

ABOUT THE AUTHOR

Ms Gladness Katega supports women who face trials in life learn how to overcome challenges, "rise from pain to purpose" through her movement "Queen Unleashed" and provides business coaching for female entrepreneurs through her organization Iamwomanpreneur Ltd to women worldwide.

Gladness has served women internationally providing business consultancy services and personal development support. She empowers women to follow their dreams and passions despite challenges that life may throw at them & discover their purpose.

Gladness is a business consultant for over 10 years with a passion for entrepreneurship development in Africa. she lives a purposeful life of supporting women to unleash their full capacity through her social enterprise "Unleash Yourself With Gladness CIC" with her programs, courses, coaching, workshops & annual conferences & Queens Retreats.

BOOK ENDORSEMENTS

I n this book, Gladness Katega has been able to articulate the importance of becoming self aware in order to unleash the gifts deeply buried within us. She has shown us throughout the chapters that there is another side of pain that very few people manage to explore. When one perseveres to the end, the reward is covered with endless possibilities. This is a great book to have in your library. It's time for all Queens to be unleashed!

Joyce Marendes − CEO of Breaking Limitations LLC

In my humble opinion, QUEEN UNLEASHED by Gladness Katega − recognized internationally as a business leader, motivator, women empowerment advocate provides much needed answers in these times. Her story is the embodiment of tenacity, grace and overcoming obstacles. What touched me about this book is the sheer transparency and practical steps to breakthrough. I believe this book will be used for years to come as blueprint to helping people to unleash the greatness within.

Dr Joe Benjamin – www.JoeBenjamin.org

I respect Gladness for taking the courage to show us her wounds. Do you know why Jesus showed his disciples his wounds? It because wounds minister deeper than crowns and accolades. My mentor says that " The Broken Become Masters At Mending,

Most people envision the prize without being cognisant that it comes with a price. The best of God's Generals have been furnished in The Furnace of Affliction. Those have climbed highest, have often come from their lowest. A testimony without a test becomes a boast-mony

This book will help so many people to transform their pain into purpose. A must read indeed!

Bishop James G. Maina - Founder The School Of Wisdom

If you are stuck in your life, know you want more or deserve more, then this book is a must read. Gladness wrote this book out of fresh, raw perspective. It entails how she was able to discover her purpose to unleash her best life. If you are looking for a way to unleash the greatness locked in you, then this book is a must-read for you.

Titilayo Owolana MRPharms - CEO Matamba Limited www.matamba.org

I love the simple yet powerful way this book has been written. Gladness opened our eyes to what is within us and how we can activate it to be everything we were created to be. The world is waiting on us to be unleashed and Gladness has given us a step by step method we can use to do that effectively and efficiently.

You have been designed and destined for more than where you are right now because you have what it takes to make it. Keep smiling and keep shinning!

Tunji Olujimi – Book Author Coach and Publishing Consultant – CEO of Accelerated Authors Academy

www.acceleratedauthorsacademy.com

CHAPTER 1
INTRODUCTION

"My Daughter is my Testimony, The Awakening of my Story"

By Gladness Katega

As a young lady, I had always seen myself as a strong and beautiful black confident woman who has so much to offer and value to give, and nobody could deny my existence in their presence. I was so sure of my identity growing up in life that I often told myself "nobody could take advantage of me". I was always the most vibrant in the room, but somewhere along the line of life, I must have lost this side of gladness as I ended up losing myself and making terrible decisions in my life. But thank God for his mercy and grace that I can write this book today, having received wholeness and rediscovered myself again and Unleashed the Queen inside of me.

During my early twenties, I grew up to be a beautiful and pleasant young lady, my degree studies gave me the confidence, character and charisma to stand on stage and deliver a presentation without fear. I considered myself a smart girl as I had answers to every question and discovered my gift of writing during my master's degree. When put on the spot, I could write up 2,000 words essay in an hour. I was the life of a party and my opinion was the most sought-after in small groups. I thought life was going to be bliss with the attributes I possessed as a young lady in my mid-twenties.

Then, there was the season I participated in beauty pageants, that was a time to remember. 2017 was the highlight of my twenties as I won Miss Tanzania UK, becoming the first-ever titleholder, this is one of my proudest moments. This was the beginning of what I like to call my "purpose journey" as I walked into the competition on the last day and took the crown.

I had a great experience participating in the national Miss Tanzania beauty pageant competitions in Dar es salaam, but this was not my dream life. I finished off with being in the top 10 and didn't pursue it further.

This time in my life was the beginning of my revelation to the purpose that God had for me and Tanzania, as today I have businesses in my home country. That year, little did I know that I was experiencing what was to become a profound moment of my identity as a Tanzanian woman living in the UK.

Today, I have a passion for supporting entrepreneurship development in Africa. I connect people with the resources and opportunities for economic enhancement and I also connect them with people in the diaspora with prospects to do business in Africa. By the year 2020, I have become an international speaker, author, serial entrepreneur, Busines & Personal coach. I run an international business and on the verge of launching a ministry through this book "Queen Unleashed CIC".

Back to my twenties, whilst everything seemed fantastic on the outside as a young lady, all was not well on the inside, unknown to me at the time I had internal wounds that were playing a huge role on the decisions I was making in my personal life.

I began dating men just to fill the void of an absent father, I was seeking love and security from the male species because I didn't grow up having the kind of love I needed as a child that you would get from a father figure. My mother was a hard-working single woman who did so well taking care of me and my younger sister on her own. Like most black single mothers, she worked round the clock to provide for our every need. She had come into the UK with nothing but studied hard and qualified to be a professional nurse enabling her to give us a comfortable life.

My mother's hectic work life meant she wasn't available to give us the emotional support that we needed while growing up, but we were happy children. This resulted in me falling for the wonderful words of any man that said they loved me and showed me affection that I wasn't getting at home.

At the age of 24, I was engaged to a young man who was not even my "type". Soon as I realised this, I broke it off, only to end up falling for a man that chased me from the age of 18 but was worst then the last one I was committed to throughout my 20's. This newfound love of mine with "John" -for this book-, seemed like everything that I needed in life at the time. I fell for the typical stereotype "tall, dark and handsome". He appeared to have great dreams and ambitions for our future and he lavished me and my family with gifts. He seemed to have all the money to take care of my needs, or so he wanted me to believe. That's pretty much all I took into consideration when choosing a man in those days.

January 2010 I got engaged to him, and it wasn't the proposal I had ever imagined because I was away from my family. He took me to his home country for a visit on a holiday and I was feeling on top of the world. One week into our holiday, John put an engagement ring on my finger one morning and we got married at the local registry a few days later. Everything was happening so fast, I didn't even have a moment to think things through. John suggested we get the legal marriage done whilst in his home country due to various reasons that he explained to me at the time. Little did I know this was the beginning of a disaster.

When I got back home to London from what was initially a holiday in Johns home country, I return as a married woman. A few months later, I found out that I was pregnant. Things were moving super-fast and to be honest, I feel like I have had amnesia because I can't recall very well the things that occurred in that season with John. What I do know is, because I was pregnant, my family suggested we have an "official" white wedding as soon as possible because it would be an embarrassment for me to give birth outside church wedlock.

So I became a wife and a mother whilst studying for my business degree and trying to figure out what I wanted to do with my life. All of that was put on hold as my new role meant that I focused on being a mother and a faithful wife according to my then husbands views and school of thought.

The first few years of marriage were wonderfully exciting as we built a family together and all was well until I started discovering me. My passion for business began to haunt me as I wanted to explore entrepreneurship. I didn't know what I wanted for my career at the time, but I knew I wanted to do more with my life than just have kids and be a housewife.

After 4 years of marriage and 2 children, It seemed that we did not have the same opinions about the role of a wife. Pursuing my master's degree was an issue to John as he believed it would distract me from being a mother and supporting his career. At the time, I was assisting him with his businesses. Everything changed between us since we no longer saw eye to eye on many issues in our marriage and life in general. When I found Christ and focused on church, it became apparent that even our faith in God was at different levels. We had different opinions about how to practice our faith and raise a family.

All in all, my marriage developed huge cracks that nobody could fix. I became unhappy and unfulfilled and there was no one to talk to. Being the eldest child from my parents, I was the example that my siblings were looking up to. So,

I moved on with life and John did too. We were not living as a married couple, we just co-habited. I focused on pursuing entrepreneurship and setting up a business to get away from the chaos in my matrimonial home.

What I didn't realise at the time was that this problem would not just go away or fix itself. It would either get worse or I choose to change my life and save myself from a lifetime of pain. The later was not an option for me at that time. I continued to manage my situation, pretending that I was happy and I prayed for 4 years that God should change John. What I have learnt now is that God cannot change anybody that is not ready to change themselves and John was not up for any changes whatsoever.

I'm not here to speak for him or make excuses for myself. What I know now is that this particular man was not the right one for me because we differed in values, thought & belief, lifestyle, culture, vision and purpose. We did not want the same things in life and the biggest mistake I made was getting into a marriage without identifying my core values, beliefs, vision and most importantly discovering my purpose. So I ended up with somebody I was unequally yoked with, deceiving myself with the popular notion "opposites attract". That's nonsense!

You should never get married before knowing yourself and understanding your needs and desires. The most important thing in life after your relationship with God is knowing your identity in God. Understanding who you are will help you discern and attract the right person for you in alignment with your purpose in life.

After 8 years of marriage, I finally had the revelation that its either I officially get divorced and leave the toxic relationship or continue cohabiting and living in denial. I had to chose to either deny myself of living a purposeful life or set myself free and leave the broken marriage.

So I finally decided to leave and went away on holiday with the kids to clear my mind. I planned to come back and process my divorce but I didn't know this was the beginning of stepping into my purpose calling. Whilst on holiday in Tanzania on 8th January 2019 my first daughter Amore passed away at 7 years old. Unfortunately, she caught an infection and her body failed to fight it. Amore had a low immune system, she was sickle cell anaemia from birth and her death was the most traumatic thing to ever happen to me in my entire life!

I came back to London hurt, broken and so confused, wondering how God could allow this to happen to me. Why now? When I was just about to start a new life, "why lord why?" I questioned and cried for many nights for the first few weeks, baffled and confused and in great disbelief about what had happened. Then, as we prepared for Amore's funeral, many people stayed with us at my mum's house. My brother, sisters, cousins, uncles and aunties from the UK came to grieve the death of my daughter. I still prayed that she would wake up from the dead and did not accept her passing until she was laid into the ground. Whilst funeral arrangements were being made, I was in complete denial of her passing to Glory. I barely ate and kept to myself just waiting for the miracle to happen "she will wake up soon", I told everybody.

Around 3 days before the funeral, my sisters prayed for me and we worshipped all night. The next morning, I woke up feeling encouraged to live again and look after my kids. I woke up to give my kids breakfast as my sisters who normally monitor me had left to sort out funeral arrangements. I assured them I was okay to be left alone and they could see a difference in my attitude. That morning soon as I and my kids left my bedroom, I heard an explosion. A fire had lit up in the room, the bed and curtains caught fire, the mattress, wardrobe, carpet and everything burnt to ashes. As the fire brigade came to handle the situation, I couldn't help but think, what if I was still sleeping like I had been doing for the past few weeks? What if I hadn't woken up the kids for breakfast? Thoughts exploded in my mind. That day, I knew that God had saved me for a reason. The fire might have been an accident but the escape I had was not coincident. I am convinced that God had a plan for my life and whatever the enemy meant for evil, this was the beginning of my turn around.

The fire Forensics said that a laptop had malfunctioned and set fire to the bag where it was kept. Some would say it was witchcraft but whatever it may be, what I know is that it happened and nobody was hurt or injured. It was a wakeup call for me because I realised that with all that has happened, it could still have been worse.

Moving forward to a few months later, I was finally set free from the toxic marriage. The incidents that happened between me and my ex-husband after my daughters funeral, I cannot even put to Ink. However, a revelation occurred and I moved out with my kids and started a fresh life after 9 years of marriage. The next few months were the best months of my life as I regained my self-esteem, renewed my strength, discovered my true self and learned about my identity in Christ. I now realised that the life I was living was not God's plan for me. I had decided without consulting God which led to a broken marriage, but he assured me that he would turn around everything for my good. This is because he has a purpose for my story to impact others and transform lives.

I would say 2019 was the most challenging year of my life. I went through brokenness, divorce, loss of a child, homelessness and real identity crisis in one year. On the other hand, I would say 2019 was the best year of my life as I "Unleashed myself with Gladness". It was the year of transformation in my life where I left the darkness and saw the light.

I do not understand why things happened the way they did, but I am not here to understand or change what I cannot control. What I do know is that God is my creator, he has a plan for my life. No matter the decisions that I had made, if I follow his word, he will make everything work out for my good.

The new decade began and the real "Gladness "was revealed. I started the year 2020 in church and I remember as we counted down to midnight, I felt a physical shift in my spirit, body, mind and soul. I was a new Gladness, transformed and my identity had changed from broken to brilliant. I spent the year learning about my values, beliefs, capacity and realised my identity as a Queen. This was the start of my abundant life; I shared my testimony to the world and soon realised how blessed I was to have concurred the battles I faced in the past 10 years. I had a revelation of my purpose from God to support women, help them discover their true self and overcome challenges by rising from pain to purpose.

Hence, I write this book to share my testimony. So that you can be encouraged to see life challenges for the lessons they bring and learn from them, as opposed to becoming bitter and fail from them. If you are facing a challenge, you too can rise from pain to purpose by seeking God to reveal to you the purposeful life he has in store for you.

In this book, I have outlined some of the key things that I learnt and strategies that I implemented to help me unleash my true identity and discover my purpose through my pain. I trust that this book will bless you and help you realise your true identity and purpose. If you can implement the steps in this book and also seek God, he will reveal to you the purpose of your life. Awake, Arise, Activate, Action, Achieve!

CHAPTER 2
AWAKE

Dear sleeping beauty it's time to wake up & face reality....! Gladness x

Rising from pain to purpose begins with an awakening experience. This is a recognizable moment in time where everything shifts in your perspective and you realise the hidden truths about your life. You awake the moment reality hits you on the one thing in your life that you avoided dealing with for a very long time. The Awakening is your moment of revelation where you wake up from your deep sleep of idealism to realism. You suddenly become aware of what you have to do to transform your life for good.

You will know you have experienced an awakening when your perspective changes. It will be like a blind man that finally sees and goes from darkness to light. If the change you go through is not that specific and your views to a matter have not converted to something different, then you haven't had an awakening experience.

After awakening, you feel like you have been living in a bubble all of your life which has just burst wide open. Now you can see everything. An awakening experience is like you have been rebirthed into somebody new, as you leave behind the false views that you had about life and you begin to see the truth. Your awakening will have you review your thoughts and impressions about people and situations. You will become enlightened to see things for what they are.

As you awake, your attitude will change, your thoughts and mannerism even the way you speak will change. You won't recognise yourself for the person they tell you that you used to be whilst you were in the bubble. However, you will be able to recall the incidents that happened before your awakening.

I had my awakening after my daughter's funeral in early March 2019, when I didn't recognise the man I had been married to for almost 10 years. I realised that he was a narcissist. My awakening made me realise I was in a mentally abusive relationship and by this point, he was accusing me of killing my daughter. He would come to my house and make loud proclamations, blaming me for our daughters' demise during the holiday with the kids in Tanzania. He looked at me boldly in the eyes and said "you killed her", I will never forget the pain I felt when he said these harsh words to me. The truth is, I went on holiday with the kids because I wanted to get away from him, having found out that he had 4 other children with another woman in his home country. When I found this out months before my travels, I had made up my mind to finally file for a divorce. I needed an escape to avoid losing my mind, so I took my kids for a planned holiday to clear my head. I travelled with the kids and he wasn't happy with the idea, hence why he says it's all my fault and "I killed her". Only the grace of God kept me sane in that season.

The moment of awakening may come to you through a series of events in your life such as a traumatic occasion like what I experienced in the passing of a loved one. Other times, an awakening may come in a message that touches your heart and it will feel like the person was talking directly to you and it wakes you up and out of the bubble you were stuck in, back into reality. You will know it has happened because your perceptions will change, you will start seeing things differently to how you have been seeing them and you will have sudden clarity about the confusion you have been facing for a long time.

The moment you have an awakening, it's important to accept the new reality that you have recognized. For me, this realisation was that I am married to a narcissist who does not love me, lied to me before marriage and has another family that I knew nothing about for 10 years. Once I accepted this truth, I knew that I have to come out of the toxic relationship before it's too late. The behaviour of the man I was calling my husband was dangerous, so I started planning my exit.

The truth is, I already knew he was unfaithful for years during our marriage and had my suspicions about his dealings in his home country. I was doing my investigation, but I never expected a whole other family. My marriage was over 3 years before this revelation, but I never had the guts to file for a divorce. I was worried about what people would say which sadly had me living an inauthentic life. The truth was clearer when my daughter died as I could see the similarity in the children my husband had to my children. If this hadn't happened, I probably would have still been in denial till now. I am heartbroken by the passing of my daughter, but I know that God allowed it to happen for a reason. My awakening would not have occurred if this traumatic event didn't happen, so my daughter is my testimony of freedom and the reason I live a purposeful life today.

An awakening is meant to set you free from entrapment and reposition you to discover your purpose in life. The choice is yours as God will not force you to do anything that you are not ready to do. I would not be living the purposeful life that I am living today had I chosen to stay in denial. I could have carried on for another 10 years with a man that doesn't love me or support my growth, but I realised that my sanity is more important than marriage. Most importantly, it was clear I could not accomplish purpose whilst married to that man. So if you are in a similar predicament, the question I have for you is; will you choose your purpose or marriage?

Your awakening is a journey of self-awareness, you will discover your true self if you come to full acceptance of your new reality by dealing with the pain in your life. You cannot accomplish your life ambitions or dreams without dealing with your internal issues on self-awareness. Failure to awake will have you living life as a "dreamer" that never really has the confidence or capacity to manifest their dreams into reality. This is such a sad truth for many women in today's society. My prayer for you reading this book is that you encounter an awakening so that your vision becomes clearer as you look into your heart and search your soul to discover your true desires.

QUEEN UNLEASHED STRATEGIES

How to activate your Awakening.......!

* retrace your steps on how you have arrived at where you are today, in that pain?

*be honest with yourself on your contribution to the painful situation you are facing...

*accept the truth of what your spirit & soul is revealing to you ...

What to do after your Awakening....

*Stay calm and don't make rushed decisions, take your time and think things through...

*Keep your thoughts to yourself until you're in full acceptance of reality

*Make a note of your feelings and revelations so that you remember everything

*Spend time in prayer daily and seek God's guidance on how to face reality

*In every
situation
learn to see
the gain not
just the
Pain!*

Gladness x

CHAPTER 3
ARISE

Dear Queen…. It's your time to shine…… ARISE!
Gladness x

Arise is the next step you need to take after your awakening. Once you have had an awakening, your life will never be the same again except you choose to accept the revelation you had. Once your bubble has busted, you need to decide to move forward and not stay stagnant, so you need to Arise!

When you have truly awakened you will no longer be comfortable with the situation as normal. You will not settle for mistreatment, abuse or people taking advantage of you. Once reality has kicked in, you will be very uncomfortable for a while with your existing surroundings in a toxic relationship.

I remember wanting to leave immediately I awoke... but there is a process that you have to follow, especially if you are living with an abusive man or he has access to your accommodation. Do not confront the situation heads on without having a proper plan. You need to prepare your mind and guard your heart through the transition of awakening. This process is rising from pain to purpose.

How you proceed from your awakening will determine which direction you go forward in life. So, you must take your time and make the right choices for you, and not for anybody else. Your sanity is the most important thing here.

You can either rise from your pain and discover your purpose or fall from your pain into depression or frustration and remain the same. How you ensure to rise and not fall after awakening is by reflecting on what you don't want to happen to your life as a result of the pain, loss or failure. Focus instead on what you desire to achieve in your life being Gods purpose.

Purpose was my main focus during my transition from pain to healing This was the key element to my rising from pain and walking into my destiny, as I unleashed into the person God created me to be as Gladness.

Rising from pain after a hurtful experience is not a simple process. You can only arise by transforming the pain into strength through the desire and hunger for change in your life. You have to want the transformation for yourself to rise from pain to purpose. It cannot be something that somebody forces or has to convince you to do, you can only arise after awakening when you truly desire it in your heart.

Girl get up!

Stop feeling sorry for yourself, it's time to get up and change your story......! Gladness x

The number one determinant of arising from pain is your ability to deal with the negative thought's in your head, which can very easily bring you down. Rising is the capacity to believe in your positive future more than your negative past. You arise by eliminating all contradictory thoughts and emotions that go through your brain, trying to keep you in that toxic environment of limitations.

As you try to arise, you will have thoughts of disbelief that will convince you to stay the same and not go through the process of changing your life. The little voices will come that tell you "you can't possibly start fresh, its hard work, you won't make it". You have to verbally rebuke these thoughts and tell yourself "I can do this, I deserve better because God has a purpose for my life".

I remember facing conflicting thoughts in my head during my rising process. I kept imaging how shameful it would be to have wasted 9 years of marriage… "What would people say about me?" I thought to myself. I kept trying to justify and rationalize the concept of staying in a marriage because it would look better for my family, my brand and it's easier than starting afresh. What motivated me to arise and choose my purpose over marriage was the desire to live a happy life. Knowing the vision that God had shown me about how a marriage ought to be, "enjoyed and not endured", gave me the strength to do the right thing of leaving the toxic relationship and disregard all discouragement.

I know it may seem easier said than done. To arise from pain is not a walk in the park. It does require courage and wilful strength but it's not impossible once you decide to love yourself enough, put yourself first and worry about the rest later. Often, failing to rise from pain is brought about by thoughts of everything and everybody else other than yourself. Broken women don't seem to think about their needs.

Women are the master keeper of everybody else's interests before ourselves, this attitude often costs us our happiness and sometimes our lives.

The truth is, most women stay in abusive relationships or situation because they haven't got the will power to leave for different reasons. This may include staying for the sake of the children, not having the financial capacity to survive on their own or culture and family won't allow them to leave etc. None of these reasons justifies staying in an abusive relationship nor equate to a personal desire to enjoy being abused. This means there is a lack of self-love and a lot of people-pleasing. Of course, one of the popular reasons I hear women give for staying in abusive relationships is because they are religious.

Women will tell you about the notion of what God has put together no man shall separate. Meanwhile, God had nothing to do with you joining hands with an abusive man. You attracted him all by yourself and never consulted God in the development of that relationship, I don't mean to be harsh but it's the hard truth.

On the other hand, maybe you prayed to God about the relationship but you never heard back or you were already broken from other traumas. Because of this, you attracted a narcissistic and will continue to experience similar toxic relationships until you deal with your past trauma.

I am not a doctor, therapist or counsellor but I qualify to speak from experience. I have been in a mentally abusive relationship for 10years with a narcissist, whom I attracted and ended up with due to childhood trauma and daddy issues. I had not addressed these issues and I've seen many women experience the same thing.

Failure to accept your trauma issues and begin the healing process from past hurts could be the detriment of your rising from pain. You may get stuck in the same place after your awakening. For you to Arise, you need to accept the reality of what you are facing and accept to do the necessary healing work to transition to the next process of rising from pain to purpose.

Trauma is a common cause for lack of rising from pain to purpose amongst women, especially in the African community. We often do not deal with childhood issues and they affect us in our adulthood without knowledge. The truth is, most of the time, men become abusers to women because of their undealt childhood trauma ranging from neglect, lack of father figure and abuse to mention a few. These are often a repetitive cycle amongst African families. So, most men act from what they have seen in their childhood. Research shows that very few men can face childhood trauma and deal with it positively to avoid repetitive behaviour. This is a problem not often discussed amongst families, peers or society. It is seen as a taboo to have such conversations in most homes.

I submit to you today, if you can trace your childhood trauma and deal with it through healing, then you can rise from your pain and into your purpose. The question you have to ask yourself is; are you ready to face the truth and unleash a greater version of yourself?

If you are a woman reading this and struggling with pain and hurt from an abusive relationship, I plead with you to face your childhood trauma. It's the key to your freedom and the beginning of rising from pain to purpose, into a life that God has ordained for you. Arise and walk into your purpose!

Its Time
to
Restructure
your life so
you can
Reach
your
Destiny!

Gladness

CHAPTER 4
ACTIVATE

Girl, switch into your power gear & Activate your inner Queen! Gladness

The awakening and rising from pain is the beginning of your transformational journey. The real work starts with activating your power within to unleash your true self into the world and start living a purposeful life into your destiny.

To activate your inner power, you need to have an understanding of the reason for your pain and how you got into the position you are in. Most importantly, if your pain is coming from a bad relationship, you need to deal with your childhood trauma, then you will be able to rise. Activating your power comes from your acceptance of a new beginning.

The activation step is where you discover the power inside of you as a woman of purpose. You will gain the strength to overcome your pain and use it to build yourself up, to become all that you were created to be by God. Your activation is released through self-identification of who you are, what you are created to do, your values, your worth, your gifts and talents. Also, know and acknowledge your beauty and flaws as a part of your identity. Understand that your experiences and failures don't define you but refine you to become all you were created to be, a blessing to the world.

To rise from pain to purpose you will go through the stages of AWAKE, ARISE, ACTIVATE and ACHIEVE, this is what it takes to Unleash the Queen inside of you and be able to walk in your God-given purpose. The completion of this process means you will go from brokenness to brilliance and successfully recreate your life to start manifesting your desires.

The process is not easy and may vary in duration depending on your capacity to overcome negative thoughts and your circumstances. However, it's not impossible no matter what challenges you have faced in life. What doesn't kill you, can only make you stronger. One thing I know for sure is that everything you have been through has been allowed by your creator to lead you to the greatest version of yourself.

In the world, we take the pain and hurt as such a negative thing, but actually, some of the greatest accomplishers in the world have risen from pain. They can testify that it's the painful experience that refined them to be able to accomplish their success.

It is known that even the most precious stone like a diamond has to undergo a lot of pressure to showcase its beauty. It is not valued by the pressure it has been through, but it's the quality of the gem that is valuable because it is a diamond stone.

The Activation process of rising from pain to purpose is about taking the negative experience and finding the lessons learnt, then turning that into an opportunity to do better and become greater.

wisdom is formed through learning and mistakes are the best teacher!
Gladness

I often say that I would not be the woman that I am today without being through what I have been through. How I value myself today has been as a result of surviving the trauma and pain of being mistreated. It's possible that had I not overcome that mental abuse, I would still have undervalued myself in so many areas of my life. I would have still considered myself an average instead of acknowledging myself as the Queen that I am.

Now that I understand my worth, my relationships are better because I attract people that value me. I have better experiences because I surround myself in positivity and so my life is better in all areas. I have overcome pain and discovered my worth.

Activation of your inner power comes with self-identification. This has to be done to complete your healing process and rise from pain to purpose. You cannot activate your inner power and strength without realising who you are as an individual. You have to be able to eliminate negativity in your mind and all other notions of self, unrelated to your true identity as God's precious daughter. You have to eradicate all things that you were told to be by your abuser and others and create a new identity for yourself like a Queen.

To activate your inner power, you need to go through the process of wholeness by healing from your brokenness, to start manifesting your true potential in life. When you have successfully risen from pain to purpose, you would have to undergo complete detoxication by healing your brokenness and being transformed into a new you. This is not something you can fake or pretend. Wholeness cannot be hidden, it will show in your appearance, character and actions to the extent that others will notice that something has changed about you. You will have a certain glow that never existed when you were broken.

Wholeness will activate your inner power, increase your confidence, transform your mindset and bring forth the manifestation of your full potential in life. So long as you maximize the use of your gifts to full capacity. It is important to heal your brokenness and seek wholeness, otherwise, your rising to purpose will be short-lived. A person that does not complete their healing process to wholeness will still have cracks of brokenness. This lives within them and like a cracked mirror it will forever distort their self-image.

A person who is not whole cannot reveal their inner power, as the brokenness will continue to attract negativity in life. The relationships you form would still be toxic and you would still attract narcissistic people because you have not dealt with the pain and hurt from your past trauma. This would not give you the confidence of having better relationships. Lacking wholeness creates a misconception about everything in life, so you see evil in everyone and every situation such that nothing good comes from what you try to achieve in life.

The sad truth is that sometimes brokenness's is unknown. It is inherited from parents or childhood upbringing that has been covered up over the years and never realized. This might seem dramatic, but it's a fact that most people suffer from childhood trauma that affects their adulthood behaviour. However, most people don't realise it unless triggered by an incident that allows them to reflect like I did when my daughter passed on. Otherwise, traumatised individuals live depressing lives and entertain abusive relationships unknown to them, due to lack of self-esteem and self-identity crisis. This is a result of something that happened in their childhood that needs healing.

We are all responsible for ourselves to protect and maintain good mental health. We should also look out for others by being sensitive to their feelings and mindful of treating them with love and respect. One of the reasons why abusive and mental health issues are rising in today's world is because the behaviour is covered and enabled by society. With myths stating imperfection as a normal thing instead of giving support to introduce change. For example, in the community when a man cheats it is often said "that's how men are" or "men will be men". These types of comments enable bad behaviour in men and make it difficult for people to seek change. We entertain this bad behaviour and then end up with repeating patterns and cycles in families of cheating men. I know that women cheat too, but here I'm dealing with the majority of women that find themselves in this repetitive cycle within their families.

We have to make change happen by starting with disallowing bad behaviour and changing the way we perceive these topics of mental health and abuse in relationships. Mental health is not a common subject in most African families and abusive relationships are on the rise in African culture, more now than ever before. So we need to speak up and make change happen. As in today's world, we seem to have learnt how to function with disfunction, by labelling people that face challenges. For instance, calling them victims, depressed, alcoholic and treating the symptoms with anti-depressants instead of dealing with the root of the problems in the society, starting with our homes.

You can't change whats going on around you untill you change what's going on inside of you!

Gladness x

Keys to Wholeness

Here are a few tips I have for overcoming pain and finding healing

- *Acceptance;* for you to receive wholeness and activate your inner power, the first thing you have to do is conduct a self-assessment. You need to acknowledge that you are broken and need healing and avoid self-sabotage through pretence. You have to trace the pain you are facing back to its root and deal with the issues that led you to your trauma once and for all. This is the only true way of becoming whole. You have to stop the blame game of pointing fingers at those that wronged you and admit to the part you played in reaching the situation you are in that has got you broken.

- *Get support:* healing may not be a process you can do on your own. It is ideal to find a trusted person that you can confide in and who can tell you the truth you need to hear to get over your pain. You need to find a person you trust to help you overcome the pain. This has to be somebody that will tell you the truth and not pamper your pain. If you can, get professional counselling or speak to a trusted leader or friend, just speak to somebody.

- *Eliminate pride:* one of the most common hindrances of wholeness is pride. This comes with not admitting your wrongs or not wanting to feel ashamed by denying what is going on. For you to receive wholeness you have to be humble and accept humiliation that you may feel within yourself, as a result of what has happened in your life. Girl, it's okay not to be ok! there is no shame in admitting pain to get your healing. You can get over this phase by feeding yourself with positive affirmations daily, as part of your transformational process. *Real power is revealed in truth.*

AFFIRMATION

Hey sis, I hope this book has been a useful tool for you to Awaken from your bubble and Arise from that painful situation, by Activating your power and go into the world to Achieve your God-given purpose in life.

I want you to know that I believe in you and I got your back if you need a helping hand along your purpose journey. Here are a few affirmations to help you get started. Don't forget to join the community *"Queen Unleashed"*

(These are good for standing in the mirror and speaking to the queen inside of you)

Dear Queen...

You have to Dust off the Dirt in your life to MANIFEST Gold into your life...

Don't be afraid to let go of what doesn't VALUE you in order not to devalue you...!

When you keep TRASH in your life, it takes up space for CLASS in your life...!

Don't worry about who understands you, focus on who QUALIFIES to be around you!

When you QUANTIFY your value and worth you won't be so bothered about the dust falling off your shirt. That is, toxic people, leaving your life.... instead you will thank God for the pain and hurt as with that comes to your purpose and your growth!

Dear Queen,

I just want wanted to let you know the crisis your facing is for your increase. So smile knowing that God is about to elevate you and trust in him for your breakthrough.

Girl, it's time to get up from that victim mentality, put on your shoes and step into your purpose...!

Queen it's time to Unleash!

Yes, I know you were abused....

Yes I know you are in pain, it hurts...

Yes, I know they mistreated you...

Yes, I know they manipulate and use you...

Yes, I know they left you with nothing....

Yes, I know you wasted years of your life...

And I understand that you are all on your own...

And you got kids to look after by yourself....

And you haven't got money to do what you want to do...

But Girl, you got God and he's all you need to start again.. believe me he comes through and if he did it for me he can do it for you too..!

But first, get up, stop the pity party otherwise, this time next year we will be having this conversation again. Girl!...don't let that be you.

Step Out Now & Rediscover Yourself!

Girl, you are a Queen, so go out and Rule your Kingdom!

Dear Queen,

DESTINY doesn't come easy you got to do the NECESSARY...

it's time to Kiss away the Pain and Walk into your PURPOSE.

Are you ready?

Dear Queen...

It's time to UNLEASH your true self, discover your worth, determine your Value then add Tax and do not offer discounts!

Apply in every area of your life then thank me later. X

A Queen is like a flower, she blossoms when planted in the right place and watered. But a flower cannot grow in darkness, it needs light.... Girl, its time to come into your light and shine!

Dear Queen...

Do Learn to fall in love with yourself, it's the key to unveiling your value and inner wealth

If you don't love yourself, you May find out that they say they love you, but not value you because you have not discovered your inner wealth.

"Loving yourself is setting an example of the kind of Love you want to receive"

The only constant thing in life is CHANGE. the key to SURVIVAL is being able to adapt to change and swiftly MOVE forward!

"You can MANIFEST your dreams, all you have to do is BELIEVE and be disciplined enough to receive it.."

Go out and shine like the goddess that you are, because you're just one step away from breakthrough... If you believe it then you shall receive it, as with your thoughts shall be the manifestation of your reality"...

Sometimes you have to go through the turbulence to get to your destination. If you try to avoid it, you May just miss your destination... because your DESTINY lies in you OVERCOMING the turbulence...

In the process, just remember that God will not give you what you cannot handle and what cannot kill you will only make you stronger...!

The sky is not the limit it's just the beauty showcasing the opportunities to explore... the only limit you have is yourself!

Printed in Great Britain
by Amazon